I0006981

How to Achieve Network Security: Using Risk Assessment and Game Theory to Protect Your Systems

Wolf Halton

Atlanta Cloud Technology Publishing

How to Achieve Network Security:

Using Risk Assessment and Game Theory

to Protect Your Systems

Copyright © 2019 Atlanta Cloud Technology

(http://atlantacloudtech.com),

Wolf Halton (https://wolfhalton.com)

All rights reserved. No portion of this book may be reproduced in any form without permission from the publisher, except as permitted by U.S. copyright law. For permissions contact: infosec@cybernightmares.com

Atlanta Cloud Technology, Inc. Atlanta GA (https:\\AtlantaCloudTech.com)

Photo Credits (c) 2018 Nelson Jones / TOPOP Entertainment Co.

This handbook is not intended to replace

professional consultation by a reputable information security practitioner. The contents are written with intent to suggest strategic approaches to help the reader to improve and supplement their professional cybersecurity posture. Every effort has been made to ensure that the content provided herein is accurate and helpful for our readers at publishing time. However, this is not an exhaustive treatment of the subjects. No liability is assumed for losses or damages due to the information provided. You are responsible for your own choices, actions, and results. You should consult reputable information security practitioner for your information security questions and needs.

Acknowledgements:

A book takes a lot of work behind the scenes, and I would like to thank Morgan Dragonwillow, William Fadul, and Mark Zupo for their unceasing support.

Table of Contents

Introduction

Now, more than ever, leaders such as yourself must incorporate heightened awareness of cybersecurity into your daily life. Many things can be automated, and there are people who may be hired to keep breaches to a minimum in your offices. This handbook is intended to alert you to a surprising amount of control you can assert in the seemingly unending cyber-barrage on your networks, your company and personal devices, as well as your clients' personally identifiable information.

Last year, hundreds of data breaches occurred in every industry, from banking to medicine, and the networks controlled by your vendors. As you know, there is a "bright line" beyond which your organization must alert your clients when a certain number of records are exposed. Many smaller breaches do not hit the media, and are reported only to the Federal and State authorities.

Over the last decade, there have been three factors present in 80% of the reported data-breaches. These factors are:

- Stolen or Weak Passwords
- Weakly Authenticated Administrative Access
- Missing Security Patches for Software or Operating Systems

It should be obvious that these three areas are the most ripe for research and remediation. My question to you is, "Why have these three factors been allowed to remain in these days of increased scrutiny by the government, the media, and the public?" Why are these issues at all? With all the billions we spend on security solutions, why haven't these factors been eradicated?"

The main reason why these issues remain current and so dangerous is that they are not actually technical issues. They are all behavioral issues. I do not intend to tear down and rebuild the Information Security Industry with this one book, but I do intend to make you aware that there are several simple things you can do personally, and in company policy to reduce these factors in your future, this year, without requiring a huge budget reorganization.

Why should you listen to me?

I have been in Information Technology roles

since before there was a named IT Industry. I have a Master's Degree in IT Project Management and Leadership with a focus on Information Security. Later I have been consulted with my College to create graduate degrees (Master's and PhD) in IT Security. I have been lead author of four textbooks, a course, and about a dozen articles about the nuts and bolts of how systems are compromised (hacked). I spent six years working my way up from adjunct to acting chair of the School of Computer Networking at a technical college in Atlanta

GA, where I taught penetration testing,

Python programming, and operating

systems. In the last few years I have worked

with large companies in the Financial and

Communications Industries as a Principal

Security Architect, focused generally on

Compliance and Policy.

This book is for you

- If you own a small or mid-sized business
- If you are a team manager, or a department director (including the CISO or the CIO)
- If you do not work in an IT team, but use computers or mobile devices in the course of your work or home life
- If you work in a highly regulated

industry
- If you have access at any time to patient medical records or to client financial records
- If you have access to employee records (including your own)

This book may not be for you

- If you never use a computer or a mobile device to get on the Internet
- If you represent any specific technical solution
- If you are looking for ways to hack into computer systems (for this you need to get a copy of "Kali Linux: Windows Penetration Testing" by Halton and Weaver (2nd Edition 2018)."

How Hackers Think

As mentioned in the introduction, there are three factors that have been found in over 80% of breaches reported in the last ten years. In this guidebook, you will learn how to strategically reduce your exploitable vulnerabilities using strategic thinking rather than tactical point solutions.

Factors:

- Weak or Stolen Passwords
- Insecure Remote Admin Access
- Unpatched Systems

Hackers think about the world

differently than other people do. Most people think in generally linear ways. Hackers think in **recursive** ways, returning to a target many times, and recombining ideas many times in many ways. This book is arranged around four intersecting domains of thought: showing the *Action* that a user takes, the usual *Justification* for making an insecure choice, one or two of the *Vulnerabilities* that a hacker could exploit based on the victim's logic, and a simple, cheap *Solution* to derail the exploits and close the vulnerability.

Action:

- The Set-up that leads the user to take dangerous shortcuts
- Expected End Result - This is a purpose that a person might have. For instance:
  - Printing remotely
  - Logging in to a web app
  - Manage list subscribers
  - Read and answer email

Justification:

- User (Victim) Logic:

  This is a common fallacy, error, or

  misunderstanding that opens a

  vulnerability. For instance:

  - That only happens to other people

- I don't keep much data
- I will only be in there for a minute
- Security is not my job

Vulnerability:

- Hacker (Red Team) Logic:
  - Find new or old way to attack a weakness in your network.
  - It is a numbers game. I don't have to find all your vulnerabilities – just one or two.

  - The more data I have on your business, the more hidden attacks are revealed.
  - Access is the first step. Securing access can be quick and automated.
  - We can combine several attacks at once.
  - We are always looking for a way in.

Solution:

- Defender (Blue Team) Logic:
    - An action that the user can take to avoid becoming a victim
    - An action that the user can take to reduce attack surface
    - Behavior that confounds hackers
        - Explaining the Security Environment by a Game or Sports Analogy instead of a Military Analogy
        - Assuming you are *not* in hostile territory is a mistake
        - Don't take things personally (that clouds your reason)

Applying Game Theory to Security

Most security vendors use military

analogy and technical jargon to sell their

solutions. The military analogies make consumers more frightened of the processes involved, and encourage them to believe and trust the vendors as keepers of the technical stuff that can mean the difference between winning or losing a battle, or a war. The situation is more like semi-automated dodge-ball than a military operation. For the sake of differentiating the sides in the game, I will refer to the network owners, managers and security teams as the **Blue Team**, and a host of players attempting to misuse the Blue

Team's networks, facilities, and devices as the **Red Team**. These are simplified labels, and I have written more exhaustive description of the motives of the groups and organizations who will be lumped into each group.

All games have rules and win conditions. There are win conditions in the security environment, but they are not symmetrical. The skill-sets of hackers are often the same on the offensive side and the defensive side. When Blue Team players focus only upon their skills in defense, they will always be playing catch-up. Blue Team

Players need to be able to think about the

game from the Red Team's point of view to

close vulnerabilities before the offense finds

them.

Football provides a great analogy to

the hacking game. When you are in defense,

you are going to tend to think in terms of

blocking. It might not occur to you that you

could let the opposing team quarterback

past your blockers on the line of scrimmage

to collect more information about the

strategy the offense is using. Have

linebackers tackle the quarterback. When you think in sports analogies, you are free to come up with more creative defenses. Some of these defenses could be designed to push the line forward.

The defensive team may be required by law or convention to ignore the solution most 2nd-year IT Security students think of - find the hackers' computers and "hack back". There are other ways to get information about the offense, that can stop them just as cold, that do not require the defense to break the rules.

- You can analyze the attacks and the code used in an exploit to find out more about the offense.

- You can contact the FBI for help with analyzing the attack (especially if the attack was successful).

- You can bring in a special team to analyze or augment your defensive line.

There is a persistent myth that defenders must defend against every possible exploit. This leads to exhaustion on the defenders' part, and an inability to separate what is important from what is

not.

If everything is "CRITICAL!!!" then in reality nothing is.

We are surrounded by irrelevant alerts. You probably remember how you felt for several weeks after the terrorist attack on the World Trade Center, and the Pentagon on 9/11? I still remember exactly where I was when the announcement came up on the TV. My little sister lives in New York City, and I couldn't reach her by phone after the event. Was she ok? Had she been

near the crash site? I had to unpack my

feelings about it to be able to function at all.

Then I unpacked the situation:

- Probably everybody was trying to call their loved ones in NYC to check on them, and the circuits were busy.
- My sister didn't live very close to the crash site and she worked in a different Borough.
- She would probably call Mom first, when she could call.
- Mom didn't live in NYC, so the signal to her would be clear.
- If something had happened to my little sister, Mom would let me know.

At that point I went on with my day.

Everybody I talked to for the next 2 weeks

seemed a little shocked, even if they had no

family near any of the crash sites, or on the planes. It was a personal attack on each of us, and we all reacted emotionally first. It may not surprise you that many of my students claimed that their emotional state, from watching the planes crash into the buildings over and over, as displayed on every station through the day, made it impossible for them to complete their homework the day before.

After a few weeks, I started thinking about the constant Terrorism alert status that never seemed to drop to Green Status.

I started to feel as if my emotional response was being milked for TV News ratings. Every time I turned on the news, they were rehashing that horrible day. Eventually "Code Yellow" became the new normal, and now the alert system is never mentioned. Did we ever get back to "Code Green" or are we forever changed, never to regain our innocence?

Research has shown we regain our innocence quite quickly. Being on high alert is exhausting, and all of us try to get back to "business as usual" as quickly as possible.

Thus it is not surprising that people tend to fall back to familiar habits. After the first we are a flurry of motion, trying to place solutions for as many threats as we can, but after weeks of "High Alert" we are too tired to think about protection as often. We become "Alarm Conditioned." To throw in a couple more analogies; I have lived in the South for 20 years, and one of the main factors leading to loss of life in hurricanes is that residents do not take the evacuation notices seriously. I learned as a volunteer firefighter, that a major cause of injury and death in structure fires is that people

overestimate the time they have to react.

For instance, "I have to get this report done

by noon, and the fire alarm that just

sounded is probably a false alarm. I'll just sit

here and grind out this report."

Data breaches happen less often than

structure fires, but they happen far more

often than terrorist attacks, however you

parse the data. There is a real probability

that your company's network will be

breached. That probability is between 50%

and 70% depending upon what source you

read.[12] Do you feel that sometimes that there just isn't enough time in the day to maintain security, and vendors are not making anything simpler? Do you feel overwhelmed by even trying to keep up?

I don't like the practice of using fear to make sales, but some security-solution vendors monetize our fear and overwhelm:

- In the same way that social media platforms and religious organizations monetize our desire for connection
- In the same way that media outlets monetize our fear of the unknown

It is important that we understand

where we are placed in the game, and what our roles are. The marketing stories used by security companies, since the 1970s, to sell all sorts of security solutions was taken from the Western movie genre of the 20th Century. Bad guys had black hats, good guys had white hats, and people who were only incidentally on either side had other colors of hats. The early silent films were in black and white, so the incidental players' hats were perceived as grey. Illustration 1 is an example from Alfred Basta & Wolf Halton (2007) of the much simplified motives by hat color that were common at

the time. Because the concept was simple

and easy to visualize, many people

embraced it. I still occasionally hear of what

I am calling Red-Team members being

referred to as Black Hat Hackers, and there

is a popular annual information security

conference in Las Vegas called Black Hat.

	White Hat Hackers	Grey Hat Hackers	Black Hat Hackers
M o t i v a t i o n	Learning new things, Protecting the network in their charge from intrusion or damage, Maintenance of the Status Quo, Work with official sanction from official organizations.	Fame, credit for solving challenging network puzzles, They are more interested in damage than pillage. Cracking firewalls so they can deface the websites of their victims is more interesting to them than making money doing it. Hacktivists who deface websites and networks of target "evil-doers" (corporations involved in the fur trade, tobacco sales, abortion, etc) are part of this group.	Cash payments, Injury to others, Stealing trade secrets, credit card numbers, customer lists, employee lists. They want whatever information they can find that will make them a profit, and offer them later profit from hitting the same organizations again. They work with unofficial sanction from official and unofficial organizations

Fig 1-h-1

Illustration 1: Simplified Motives

The Hat Model was not at all predictive, in any scientific way, and sheds no light on the question of why a person might gravitate toward using their skills in destructive ways rather than in constructive ways. Illustration 2 is a more useful and predictive taxonomy and description of the motives that drive security professionals in both Red-Team roles and in Blue-Team roles (Basta & Halton, 2007).

Taxonomy & Description	Taxonomy & Description
Novice	Old guard hackers
Limited computer and programming skills.	Appear to have no criminal intent.
Rely on toolkits to conduct their attacks.	Alarming disrespect for personal property.
Can cause extensive damage to systems since they don't understand how the attack works.	Appear to be interested in the intellectual endeavor.
Looking for media attention.	**Coders**
Cyber-Punks	Act as mentors to the newbies. Write the scripts and automated tools that others use.
Capable of writing their own software.	Motivated by a sense of power and prestige.
Have an understanding of the systems they are attacking.	Dangerous — have hidden agendas, use Trojan horses.
Many are engaged in credit card number theft and telecommunications fraud.	**Professional criminals**
Have a tendency to brag about their exploits.	Specialize in corporate espionage.
Internals	Guns for hire.
a) Disgruntled employees or ex-employees	Highly motivated, highly trained, have access to state-of-the-art equipment.
May be involved in technology-related jobs.	**Information warriors/cyber-terrorists**
Aided by privileges they have or had been assigned as part of their job function.	Increase in activity since the fall of many Eastern Bloc intelligence agencies.
Pose largest security problem.	Well funded.
b) Petty thieves	Mix political rhetoric with criminal activity. Political activist
Include employees, contractors, consultants .	**Hacktivists**
Motivated by greed or necessity to pay off other habits, such as drugs or gambling.	Work to eradicate or damage entities or causes they perceive to be evil
Opportunistic: take advantage of poor internal security.	Mix political rhetoric with criminal activity. Political activist
Computer literate.	Engage in hacktivism.

1-2

Illustration 2: Taxonomy of Red-Team Roles

The Playing Field

As with 3-D chess, there are many
sectors and levels to the playing field, and
the Blue Team enters the field with their
first deployment of computerized software
or hardware. At the start of play, the Blue
Team controls their own network and

devices, and they start looking for ways to make exploitation of their resources more difficult. Similarly, the Red Team players enter the game controlling their own hardware and software, but their first goals are to start developing game strategy and collecting information and resources related to the Blue Team and to the vulnerabilities that might be present in the Blue-controlled territory. There are many Blue Teams and many Red Teams involved in the larger game at all times.

The engagements are not always

straightforward. For instance, a Red Team might mount a Denial of Service exploit that would take a Blue Team web-server offline. They are doing this so that they can trick a other Blue Teams to route traffic expected to go to that web-server to a Red Team-Controlled web-server. Because most of us are human, we treat the exploit as a direct attack, when it may only be a ruse to draw defenders attention away from the real purpose of the play. It might also be a step in a multipart offense designed to give access to other, higher-value resources.

Engagements can also be synchronous or asynchronous. In today's playing field some exploits are spread to many target resources quickly and executed upon arrival to damage or steal data. Some exploits just sit quietly in the victim's network for an average of 18 months. Sometimes, like mouse-traps, these snap when the unsuspecting user takes the bait, which releases digital kinetic energy. Sometimes they sit passively surveying where you go on the Internet, collecting your contacts, or keystrokes. Then they slowly feed the data slowly out to a Red-Team controller. There are even some that are like time-bombs, and only execute when they receive some signal or some external event happens.

Example Red Team Roles and Goals

The Red Team roles include managing, experimenting, and researching vulnerabilities and finding ways to exploit them. The Red Teams have programmers to automate exploits so they can continue working while they sleep. The Red Teams have personnel managers and HR teams.

Exploiting systems is a business strategy

with guidelines and tactics, just like running

a hamburger restaurant or an online social-

media platform. There are complex

hierarchies as well as one-person shops.

The Red Team advantage is that they only

need to find one exploitable vulnerability.

Their disadvantage is a difficulty with

traditional hiring for all the roles needed.

One can't simply hire Red-Team exploit

specialists on a job board. To be honest,

many larger companies employ a group of

people who perform as an internal Red

Team to run limited attacks within their

network for the purpose of testing the Blue

Team defenders' readiness.

Example Blue Team Roles and Goals

The Blue Teams, our teams, develop

defenses and processes to guard our

sensitive data and assets. In some

organizations, there are specialized defense

squads trained to operate the complex

tools we use counter Red-Team exploits.

Defenders have an inherent advantage of a

legal support for their operations, and well-deployed defenses can render certain exploits forever useless. For instance, in the 1990s there was a denial of service exploit called "The Ping of Death." Back then, when a ping request came back with the expected data, but you still couldn't raise the website in a browser, we would say "The lights are on, but there's nobody home." If the ping returned with a "Host not found" message, it could be that the server was offline or that there was a network outage between us and the server. This helped Internet

Service Providers (ISP) guide customers who were experiencing connectivity problems.

The *Ping of Death* could be used in early gaming communities to knock other players out of the game by sending their computer a ping packet that was larger than average. The Windows 95 operating system was unable to process the larger ping packet and would refuse to just drop the unexpected and offending packet. It would knock the system off the network, and refuse to send or receive any other network traffic.

The permanent solution to the Ping of

Death was supplied by network-router

providers who were not directly affected by

the problem. They were prompted to action

because Sun Solaris (SunOS) servers also

had a similar vulnerability, and hard-

booting a server has a lot more impact than

rebooting a Microsoft Windows 95 client. It

took quite a while for the solution to be

deployed fully, but when that happened,

Red Team members stopped using the

attack. You cannot wait for the industry to

move as a whole to solve your security

problems.

Strategic Security for the Distracted

As a business professional, you are

Busy! There are never enough hours in the

day, and there is always someone asking for

your attention. It isn't your fault that you

don't track every breach that hits the news.

In these days of tailored news consumption,

you might not even hear about all the

breaches publicised, and there are just as

many that don't make the news at all. You

have many other issues to draw your

attention. Security vendors often advertise

products using *fear of loss* as the main

driver:

- What if your customer records are compromised?
- What if your employees' and coworkers' identities are stolen?
- What if you are hit with ransomware and your organization has to pay out millions in ransom to get your records back, or have to recreate years of historical records?
- What if your reputation as a professional, or your organization's reputation are dragged through the mud by Red-Team tactics?

These are all serious issues, and the

vendors provide you with a "magic pill"

(their solution) to make it all go away.

Overshared Emails

A common source from which the Red Team starts collecting information about how to attack your company, and to make the other offensive tactics easier, is overshared email. It is also easy to avoid, as you will see. There are two ways that email might be overshared.

1. Oversharing sensitive information: The sender hits *Reply All* instead of *Reply*, which can send their private message to hundreds or thousands of people on an email mailing list.

2. Oversharing addresses: A sender just loads all their contact list into the "To:" line on the email composition template.

   Either of these can lead to undesirable outcomes. It was an erroneous *Reply All* on the part of my late wife that led to me meeting her in person. I think that was a happy accident, but not all are so happy. You may inadvertently send out extremely sensitive data to a large group with a click. You might let everybody on the send know all the other addresses in the mailing list. A list of valid emails is useful to a spammer,

or a scammer.

Action:

The Sender's Motive:

There are two motives that lead to this

action:

1. You weren't paying attention, you got

   distracted, or you just hit Reply All

   accidentally. Accidents happen. Oops!

2. You have to send an email to any

   selected group, who may or may not

   be connected by function. You choose

to put the entire list in the To: field or the CC: (Carbon Copy) field in your message.

Justification:

Victim Logic:

1. Since it wasn't intentional, you may be embarrassed, or you might justify that people who were not specifically mentioned in the body of the message will not read the message you sent. Nobody ever seems to read my comments on the list. Why should

they start now?

2. You are used to putting small groups of addressees (of people connected by function) into the CC: field. What's different about putting an enormous number of emails in the CC: field? This seems harmless, especially if the people are all connected by some interest or function.

Vulnerability:

Red Team Logic: Footprinting

1. Private or sensitive messages can give

an unintended user a lot of useful

information to attack your company,

you the sender, or the intended

recipient.

2. If any one of the people in the list is an

    insider threat, or of anyone on the list

    forwards it to an unsavory person,

    then you have provided a good list for

    a *spear-phishing exploit*. Not to

    mention that it can upset people to

    have their email broadcast to

    hundreds of unknown people.

    Footprinting is a series of tactics to give

the Red Team understanding of the internal network, organizational chart, processes and procedures of a targeted victim. Knowing valid emails is just one piece of the footprinting process. Another way to think about footprinting is that it is "getting to know you." Footprinting tactics, in themselves, are not frightening things, any more than your looking for reviews for a movie or a babysitter should be construed as scary.

An *insider threat* is any person who might have a motive to hurt anyone else in the group, company or client-list for gain or unfair advantage. We generally do not wish to suspect our coworkers of ill-will or wrong-doing, but a large number of successful Red Team exploits are performed by insiders – people who already have access to the company network and who understand enough about the company's processes and procedures to steal from the company with impunity. The number of successful exploits that have an insider vector range from 50% to 80%, year after year. An insider can be malicious or merely neglectful.

Phishing is a Red-Team technique using email attack vectors and advertising malware that entices a recipient to click on a link or open a malicious attachment. Phishing messages are almost always written poorly, and that is the first sign of a Phishing attack. Spear-phishing is a variety of Phishing that target a specific company or the clients of a specific company. Spear-phishing emails are often from spoofed emails that look like standard emails you get at work all the time. They work because we are all predisposed to think of internal

users as less dangerous than external-

source users. You probably get emails from

the HR department with reminders about

aspects of your employee information, for

instance:

From:	HR
To:	Your Email Address
Subject:	"Open enrollment is almost over!"
Body:	
"Click on this link to pick your health insurance features for next year before 11/7/2019."	

Would you click on the link?

Solution:

Blue Team Logic - Protect Your

Recipients:

1. Always start a separate message when mailing to somebody on a mailing list with you. Then you cannot accidentally send to the whole list.

2. Use the BCC: (Blind Carbon Copy) field for your list of recipients.

   Use this rule: If the recipients need to know each other's emails to communicate outside of your message context, then you could put them all in the To: or CC: field. If

they do not need to communicate outside

of the context of your email, use the BCC:

field. There are probably more respectful

ways to introduce your recipients to each

other than just dumping all their emails into

one To:-field entry.

Password Issues

Passwords present a number of issues that have plagued network users since the beginning. Protected information must have some standardized access measure, and along with security certifications (showing the server that the requesting person has proper permissions to access the data) passwords are an integral part of the security authentication and authorization models in use today

Weak Passwords and Password

Sequencing

Action:

The Set-up:

You are responsible for administering a large number of sites and emails that are set up to be protected by passwords. Many organizations are reluctant to offer or allow ways to make passwords easy to remember. They require a minimum length and the password cannot be a dictionary word. This is a basic filter that can be turned on to make the average user's life more difficult. Many default settings found in business settings require that you change

the password every ninety days. There are

several ways to deal with the problem

safely, but a great many users frequently

fail to properly handle the password issue.

Justification:

Victim Logic:

- I don't think my information is important enough to be stolen or hacked.
- I need a password I can remember, so I will use the shortest password I possibly can, and reuse it in as many places as I can.

Vulnerability:

Red Team Logic:

If I can guess a password once, I will do some research on your email and try your password pattern in as many of your accounts as I can. If your credentials are included in the data stolen during a breach, I can know a lot about you and try variations of the password everywhere I can find evidence of your email account or your username.

If I can guess your social media passwords, I can start getting to know your private shares and your friends' private shares. If I can get into your email, I can process all your inbound and outbound mail to crack your life open.

Solution:

Blue Team Logic:

If you are resolutely fixed on making up and maintaining all your passwords in your head, at least avoid common password patterns, and don't choose the shortest possible passwords.

Common Password Patterns

Sequential

This is a pretty strong, and easily-recalled password, that you make easy to guess future passwords by incrementing the number each time you set a new password).

Me$op8amia1
Me$op8amia2
Me$op8amia3
Me$op8amia4
Me$op8amia5
Me$op8amia6

Common Password Patterns
Mnemonic
Using the same base password with the first letter the same as the first letter of the site-name. This can lead to many identical passwords
LHuo8hlijh# (for use on http://linkedin.com/)
AHuo8hlijh# (https://www.alasu.edu/)
THuo8hlijh# (www.tampastatebank.com/)
BHuo8hlijh# (https://www.bmcc.cuny.edu/)
ZHuo8hlijh# (for use at https://www.zephyrhillswater.com/)
GHuo8hlijh# (for use at https://mail.google.com/)

Common Password Patterns
Keyboard Walk
These are easy to remember, because they are sequential keys on your keyboard
qwertyuiop
asdfghjkl
mnbvjhfg
qawsedrftg
147852369
987654321

Did I mention you should choose

longer passwords?

Create better passwords, and use

different passwords at each site or account.

Use a password manager such as LastPass.com or an encrypted note app on your phone like NoteCrypt. LastPass is cloud-based and is an easier place to keep the passwords updated than local password app solutions. LastPass also allows you to quickly test for whether your passwords are stale or stolen in a breach. I have found this to be a useful app, and it is available for phones, tablets and computers.

- Test your personal password model with a tool such as http://rumkin.com/tools/password/passchk.php to get an idea how strong your model is.
- Make it your policy to double the

minimum password length, and use a password manager.

Stale Passwords

Action:

The Set-up:

You have protected your account with what you consider a long and complicated password. You never want to change it, or you have a set of credentials with which one server log into another server.

Justification:

Victim Logic:

With my 11-character password, I am

safe from any password-guessing attack. I am also a bit proud of myself that I can remember "_hY7&W29-_@." I don't ever want to have to remember any new passwords.

Vulnerability:

Red Team Logic:

If I happen to be able to capture your password hash by using one of many exploits, I have unlimited time to run Rainbow Table attacks and Brute-Force attacks. If I happen to find your email and password from 12 years ago on a dark web site, and you have never changed it, I will appreciate the gift of all those sites where you use that password.

Solution:

Blue Team Logic:

Change your password before a modern computer could find and test all possible passwords of that length. The PCI DSS 3.2.1 says passwords should be changed at least every 90 days. That assumes the minimum (PCI DSS recommended) password length of 8

characters.[1]

The PCI DSS is the *Payment Card*

Industry Security Council's Digital Security

Standard, which all organizations which

collect payments through credit or debit

cards must comply. It is a voluntary

compliance process, but it makes it more

likely that your claim of performing due

diligence related to payments data will be

believed when you find yourself in civil

1   PCI DSS main site. The
actual PCI DSS document is hidden behind a sign-up
form. Access is free, and I would be happy to go through
it with you. https://www.pcisecuritystandards.org/

court after a data breach.

In 2014, GA Tech researchers made the claim that 9 characters was the new minimum safe length. Don't play the numbers. Use your password-management tool and create a proper alphabet-soup password that the password-management tool remembers for you. Choose the longest password a given online app will allow you to have. 18-character passwords (or longer), changed regularly, keep you and your clients safe from all sorts of vulnerabilities.

Stolen Passwords

Action:

The Set-up:

Websites and web applications are breached far too often, and it's worse than you think. You never hear about most data breaches. You rarely find out about the full extent of the ones you hear about.

For example, medical professionals are aware that medical establishments are required to report to the Secretary of Health and Human Services, without unreasonable delay, a data breach exposes

more than 500 medical records. If the

breach exposes fewer than 500 patient

records, the medical establishment has 60

days to report the breach.[2]

Patients affected need to be notified

through First Class mail as quickly as is

practicable following a breach and no later

than 60 days after the fact, but if the

establishment is mistaken about how many

records were affected, or if they under-

2   HHS requirement to notify the
HHS about breaches.   https://www.hhs.gov/hipaa/
for-professionals/breach-notification/breach-reporting/
index.html

report for some perceived good reason, there will be other patients who are blissfully unaware of their exposure. If the breach is of 500 records or more, the establishment is required to announce it on their website for at least 60 days,[3] but many patients only contact a medical establishment once or twice a year. Those patients will only find out about the breach if it is announced on a news outlet that they follow. In these days of tailored news-feeds,

[3] HHS Patient-notification rules. https://www.hhs.gov/hipaa/for-professionals/breach-notification/index.html

the notification is even more problematic. It is not just a HIPAA-notification problem. All notification rules are squishy enough that the exposed records might be exposed for far longer than the notification period. The notification clock can only start after the establishment discovers an anomaly that leads them to suspect a breach has occurred.

Justification:

Victim Logic:

"There is no way that you can

completely protect yourself from a data breach, especially one at some other company. It is like trying to protect yourself from a meteorite strike, isn't it? It's so difficult, expensive and complicated to protect yourself, that there's no purpose to thinking about it."

Vulnerability:

Red Team Logic:

Once I acquire a set of stolen credentials, I can do all sorts of attacks and exploits from there.

- Footprinting
- Spear-Phishing
- Social Engineering
- Identity Theft

Since people are predictable in groups and also individually, Red-Team operatives might launch an attack on the victim's friends using the victim's email. A sent email can be deleted, before the victim gets to thinking about seeing whether there is an anomalous message in the *Sent* folder. Messages can also be sent from a different mail client, so that the victim never sees the sent message. If the secondary victims click on a link in an email that seems to be sent by you, and thus infect themselves with an *Internet Worm*, a *Remote Administrative Tool (RAT)*, a *Trojan Horse*, or all sorts of other unpleasant malware.

Solution:

Blue Team Logic

It is a little like a meteor strike, but more like defending yourself from thunderstorms, Consider that in the last 24 months there have been at least 412 breaches at medical facilities, resulting in 500 or more patient records being exposed[4], and weak or stolen passwords were factors in as many as 80% of those, the meteor-strike analogy may be pretty flimsy. Small businesses surveyed by Ponemon Institute in 2018 reported that 70% had experienced a cyber-attack, and only 28% considered themselves well-prepared for future attacks. Of those attacks, 40% reported they experienced breaches because of poor password practices. The average cost of a small-

4   HHS list of breaches over 500 records in last 24 months. https://ocrportal.hhs.gov/ocr/breach/breach_report.jsf

business breach was almost $400,000.00.[5]

Segment your secrets. Your house key doesn't open your company's front door, and you cannot start your car with it. This has probably never seemed like a tremendous hardship, but it has tripled your key-management process for years. It keeps your risk segmented. You might lose your car key and still feel safe in your home. In the digital world, you need the same

5   Nearly 70 Percent of SMBs Experience Cyber Attacks, Security Magazine.com, 2018, https://www.securitymagazine.com/articles/89586-nearly-70-percent-of-smbs-experience-cyber-attacks

separation of secrets. Remember a little

earlier we talked about *Footprinting*? If you

use the same email account for all web

application log-ins, you make the Red

Team's task easier. The higher the number

of places an email address gets used, the

higher the number of sites at which a single

credentials-gram could make you

vulnerable.

- Never use your work email for any other purpose than communicating work-related things to clients, vendors and coworkers. Your work email may be the most valuable one you have.

- Use one or more throw-away emails

for newsletters and social media. Create a newsletter email for the work domain if possible. If you have a newsletter email such as Wolf.Dont-Spam-Me.Halton@gmail.com then you can not only track when a Red-Team operative has stolen your credentials, but you can also tell when a site upon which you registered sells your information.

Use Multi-Factor Authentication (MFA)

wherever you can. Even if someone knows

your password, they are unlikely to know

the six or eight-digit number that the site

sends to your mobile device via SMS text.

There are several methods of MFA.

- Hard or soft token authentication: A hard token is a small device you can keep on a keychain. The token produces a secret code in an encrypted sequence that you add to your login credentials. You will never be able to guess with any accuracy what the next code in the sequence will be, and neither will a Red-Team operative. The soft token is an application that you install on your device that works the same way.

- SMS of Emailed secret code: Most of the major social-network platforms give you the option to use MFA (sometimes called 2-factor authentication (2FA)). This can give you a surprising level of comfort related to your social media.
- Your office network may have a Virtual Private Network[6] (VPN) to connect

6   When you are using a VPN, the only connection that you expose to the Internet, for a Red Team to intercept, is the VPN login. Since the MFA token code changes every 30 seconds, it is unlikely that a Red-Team operative would be able to use the session information that they capture at a coffee house or a motel lobby to attack you further. You will essentially never reuse the same token code in your lifetime.

your remote device to the office network securely. Make sure you buy a VPN solution that offers token or app-based MFA.

Check your commonly-visited sites for logged-in devices, and delete any which you don't recognize. In Illustration 4, below, there is a section near the top called "Where You're Logged in." This shows a computer running a Linux operating system, which I expected to see, as this is my development machine, from which I captured the image for Illustration 4. The next device is my smartphone, where I run the FaceBook App. This is also expected, as I am logged into the app. If I saw other devices, I could log out from the unexpected device(s). Unexpected devices could be places where you legitimately logged in, or they could be a device that you do not recognize. If you don't recognize the device, log out of the device, and change your password **IMMEDIATELY**.

Illustration 3 also shows you where you can implement two-factor authentication for FaceBook, which is one of the best ways that you can protect yourself from people guessing your passwords.

Illustration   3: FaceBook Security Page

Delete old phone numbers or emails

(which you have saved for password

recovery) from your social media sites.

These old accounts can be captured by a

Red-Team operative, and used to steal your

credentials and information over, and over,

and over. It is scary when it happens to you,

so let's just nip it in the bud, right here.

Weak Admin Remote Access

Action:

The Set-up:

From time to time, websites and applications need to be administered. It makes sense to make this as simple and straightforward as possible. RDP over TLS (SSL), or user/password admin credentials over HTTPS should make it safe enough. Hackers won't even be able to find my login page.

Justification:

Victim Logic:

Nobody I know of ever thinks to go to the admin page of my web app. It doesn't need any more protection than a simple password over HTTPS. There is nothing important on my site, and the shopping cart is hosted at a 3rd Party vendor.

Vulnerability:

Red Team Logic:

Most C.O.T.S. (Commercial off the Shelf) software, and most open-source software have known file-structures and the default admin logins are predictable. Most

of the weird, super-stealthy ports the

software companies use are also well-

known.

There are two major ways to attack a

vulnerable admin remote-access route:

- The first is to just guess the password of the web app on HTTPS. That route takes time, but it can be automated to test all of the 5000 most common passwords. The odds are good that the admin password will be in that list – especially if the default "Administrator" account is in use. HTTPS does not protect a site from an attack of this sort.
- The second way to attack the site is to set up a false wireless access point in the coffeehouse network with a name

that sounds more real than the official one. TLS 1.2 is relatively secure, unless there is a Red Team phony web access point in the network that your "Zero-Configuration" wifi card silently attaches to, or you accidentally mistake it for a valid access point. This is called a Man-In-the-Middle Attack, and it neatly gobbles up all your usernames and passwords, so even if you have a reasonably tough to crack password, the Red Team can collect it. They can also grab anything else you are sending through the connection.

Solution:

Blue Team Logic:

This is pretty easy to avoid with multifactor login, time, and locale restrictions, and *"separation of duties"*.

- **Use Multi-factor Authentication:**
This is the second time Multifactor has come up in the last ten pages. Multifactor Authentication (MFA) means that there is something besides the static username/password credentials. If you have an iPhone, you are used to the fingerprint login, which is a biometric multifactor authentication. The odds of somebody being able to match your fingerprint are slim. A pseudo-random six or 8-digit code that changes every minute is a pretty good defense against the Red Team, even if they have your username and password. A MiiM attack will be able to capture a token code on your web site, but that code will not be valid unless they log into your site immediately after you do. They will not be able to log in a minute later. You may see the term 2-Factor Authentication (TFA or 2FA), which means essentially the same thing as MFA.
- **Restrict the Devices Allowed:** Only

allow access from a specified set of MAC Addresses, or IP addresses.

- ○ The Media Access Control (MAC) address is the unique serial number of the network access Card (NIC). If you only allow access from a single MAC address to your login page, it reduces dramatically the number of automated attacks. A MAC address can be spoofed, so there is a limit to the perfection of this as a single-point solution.

- ○ Allow access only from a known IP address or range of IP addresses. If your policy is only to log in from a known IP, then your administrator sitting in the coffee house will have to log into your company's network through a VPN or some other tunneling technology to get to the administration login page. That cuts out anybody trying to find the admin page from any other location.

- **Only allow access during specific times:** If you allow access to your login page only during the administrator's usual working day, for instance Monday through Friday from 10:00 am to 7:00 pm, then even if the Red Team has your credentials and your MFA token, they have to use the credentials when your staff are more active, and the real administrator may be logging in. This makes it more difficult to stay hidden.
- **Separation of Duties:** Require manager approval for temporary variances for these rules. This helps keeps insider from becoming insider threats.
- Finally, to automate the security, and make it easier to audit for anomalous login attempts:
  - **Set up a Web Application Firewall:** A Web Application Firewall (WAF) to log all remote-admin access and notify on anomalous attempts. Depending

upon the WAF you use, it can also be set to:

- Automatically block IPs that attempt to login with non-existent administrative accounts.
- Automatically block "known-bad" IP addresses.
- Log all anomalous connections and requests.

Missing Security Patches

Action:

The Set-up:

It is important to install security patches, so when I am entirely done working I will allow them to be installed. I believe (with some evidence) that patches and updates often slow my progress down.

Justification:

Victim Logic:

Patches are so frequent (or rare) that they are more an annoyance than a blessing. They slow down my computer, and I cannot make money with a slow computer. Every time I install updates to Windows 10, it gets slower. My slow computer makes my clients angry because they have to wait longer for me to get their stuff done. If I have to reboot my computer, it takes a long time to get back to a workable desktop. I have to re-open all the things I am working on, and I will probably lose track of where I was before I had to reboot.

Vulnerability:

Red Team Logic:

The farther your levels of patching are from totally up-to-date, the more open vulnerabilities show up for the hackers to choose from. This effect is actually because researchers have had more time to find the vulnerabilities and to announce them. Once a vulnerability and exploit have been published, the Red Team doesn't have to be too fiendishly clever to use them in an automated fashion against any machine they can reach that hasn't been patched. - Consider that over 80% (possibly as much as 99%) of successful exploits are against known vulnerabilities with available

patches.

Blue Team Logic:

Solution:

- Automate patching as much as you can. Leave your laptop or workstation turned on, but in a state where an automated reboot will not steal your work. Set the operating-system patching to take place when you are not working.
- For a real production network, create a test network with machines identical to production to make sure a patch doesn't break some other application.
- Use full patches in your test network – don't waste time customizing the patch-bundle if it doesn't break anything.
- Check from time to time to see if your

computer is waiting on a reboot. Many patches require a reboot. An un-initiated patch = an unpatched vulnerability.

Epilogue

The suggestions above will make you safe from most attacks, and will not cost all that much – in some cases, the fix is a behavioral shift, and not a software or hardware shift. The cost of a breach is rising,[7] and ignoring the simple high-probability vulnerabilities in favor of the exciting zero-day attacks makes no sense.[8]

7   CSO Online, "Top cybersecurity facts, figures and statistics for 2018", 2019, https://www.csoonline.com/article/3153707/top-cybersecurity-facts-figures-and-statistics.html

8   Security Magazine, "Nearly 70 Percent of SMBs Experience Cyber Attacks", 2019, https://www.securitymagazine.com/articles/89586-nearly-70-percent-of-smbs-experience-cyber-attacks

There are many other ways to integrate security into your company culture, and to streamline your workflows or business processes to make things faster and cheaper.

Thanks for staying with me to the end of the book. As a reward for your interest, I want to offer you a special discount on a personalized gap-report for your business, to help you get your security strategy organized, and a year of Gold Membership in my Strategic Security Mastermind Group.

The Atlanta Cloud

Tech CyberSecurity System

- **What is the ACT CyberSecurity System?**

The ACT Strategic CyberSecurity System is a standards-based system to show you what you need to do to create the most effective cybersecurity program possible. Prepared by a senior security engineer from Atlanta Cloud Tech, the CyberSecurity System shows you the specific steps you need to follow to clean up your business security vulnerabilities. The CyberSecurity System initial diagnostic report will take from three to five weeks to prepare. We use the Payment Card Industry Digital Security Standard (PCI DSS)[9] as a basis for the system, and this means our report will make sense to any PCI expert. If you are required to use a 3rd-party QSA company for annual PCI assessment, the diagnostic report will reduce the amount of time and money the assessment takes.

9   The PCI DSS standards Documents reside at the PCI Security Standards Council's website. https://www.pcisecuritystandards.org/

Questions the ACT CyberSecurity System diagnostic report will answer

- Are we spending the right amount on cybersecurity?

  - Some companies have a good idea what their vulnerabilities are, but just don't take them seriously enough.

  - Some companies spend too much because they lack the skills to balance their risks against their security ROI.

- Are we spending that money in the

right places?

- o Building a wall will not stop birds from coming into your orchard and eating the low-hanging fruit.

- o Putting a mesh enclosure over the entire orchard will not stop a flash flood from tearing down half your trees.

- Are we prepared in the event of a disaster?

  - o Do we have a disaster recovery plan in place, and how often do we test the plan?

- How sure are we that our back-ups are recoverable, and how long will we be down?

- How long is it going to take to discover we have a problem?

● Is there a plan for business continuity?

- Have we designated our key employees, and do we have a succession plan in the event that one of these key employees can no longer act in that function?

- Do we have a backup site to work from if our main location is taken offline?

- ○ Do we have the proper insurance coverages?

- Do we have an asset management plan?

  - ○ Assets that are unknown or forgotten within the company can be lost or left running with no useful business purpose, wasting money.

  - ○ Assets become obsolescent. Hardware and software age out

of support, and get more
vulnerable with age. Do we have
a policy for hardware and
software lifecycle?

- Are our business practices and
procedures up to date?

  - Business procedures and
  workflows need to change as the
  business environment changes,
  with new opportunities, mergers
  & acquisitions, and changes in
  the legal landscape.

o The best practice is to maintain annual reviews, and make changes supported by standards and procedures.

The Strategic Security Gold-Level Mastermind Group

The Strategic Security Mastermind Group at the Gold Level is designed around the impact that a small group of individuals can achieve by meeting together to discuss the challenges they face in their daily work.

As a Gold Level Member

You are a member of a small but powerful group of business leaders consisting of up to twelve members who meet monthly for discussion. You have exclusive access to Gold-Level seminars monthly.

You are invited to an annual Mastermind Event where you can learn to use new strategic cybersecurity models to address emerging security threats.

The ACT Strategic CyberSecurity System current pricing is $14950, and Gold-Level Mastermind membership is $500 per month (or 6,000 per year), but since you

have come this far with me, I want to

reward you with a 20% discount on both

packages purchased together.

ACT Now for a Special Offer!

When you order your package, use the

PromoCode of **ACTGameTheory19.**

Remember to use the PromoCode of

ACTGameTheory19 so you get both the Gap

Report and one year of Gold-level

Mastermind access for a low monthly

subscription rate of $1396.67 (annual

$16760).

https://bit.ly/WolfHalton

100% Satisfaction Guaranteed

HTTPS://ATLANTACLOUDTECH.COM

www.ingramcontent.com/pod-product-compliance
Lightning Source LLC
Chambersburg PA
CBHW031224050326
40689CB00009B/1467